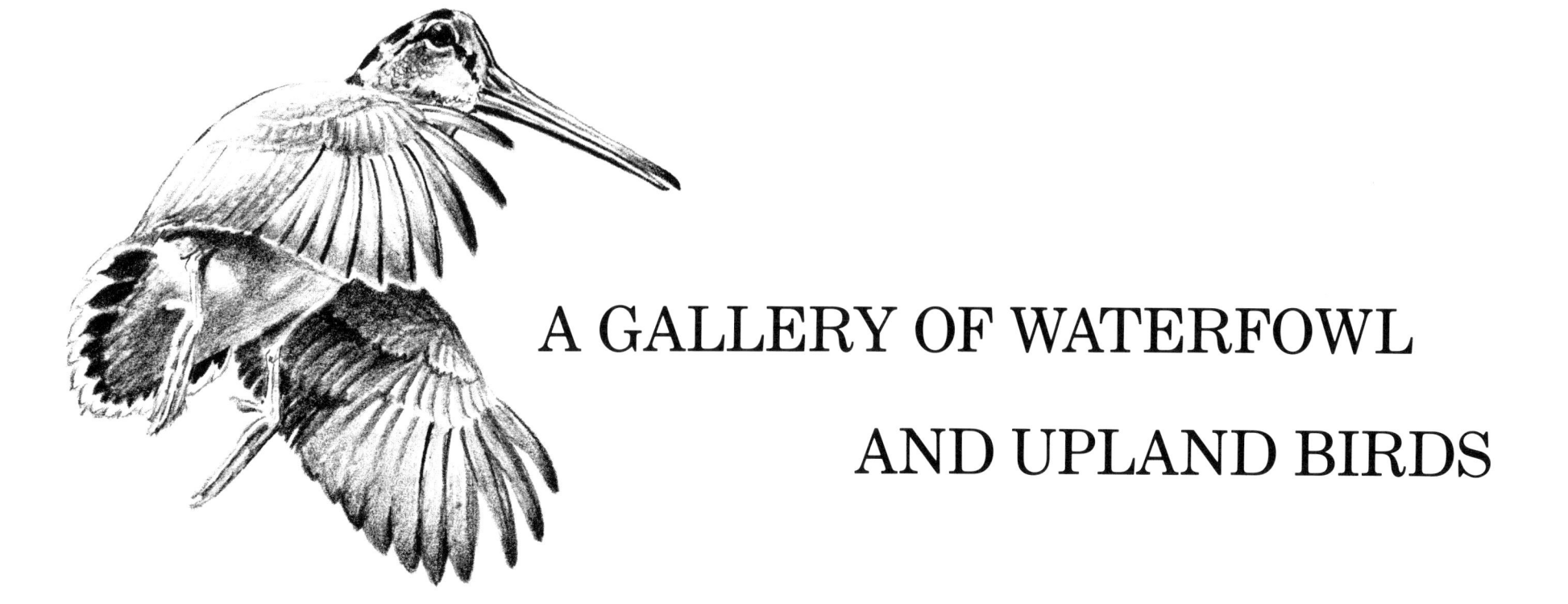

A GALLERY OF WATERFOWL

AND UPLAND BIRDS

A
GALLERY
OF
WATERFOWL
AND
UPLAND BIRDS

PAINTINGS BY
DAVID MAASS
STORIES BY
GENE HILL

PETERSEN PRINTS, PETERSEN PUBLISHING CO.
LOS ANGELES, CALIFORNIA

Copyright© 1978 by Petersen Publishing Company.
All rights reserved. No part of the contents of this book may
be reproduced without the written permission of the publisher.

Petersen Publishing Co., 8490 Sunset Blvd., Los Angeles, CA 90069

Library of Congress Catalog Card Number: 78-61769
ISBN: 0-8827-8020-8
Printed in the United States of America

CONTENTS

I
THE GAME OF GROUSE
PAGE 1

II
A BACKYARD HUDSON'S BAY
PAGE 21

III
REFLECTIONS ON THE BAY
PAGE 41

IV
VOICES FROM WOODCOCK COUNTRY
PAGE 57

V
TWO's, FOUR's and XXL's
PAGE 71

VI
WHEN PHEASANT SEASON WAS FROM CHORES 'TIL DARK
PAGE 91

VII
SHOTGUNNER'S FANCY; SHOTGUNNER'S PLAIN
PAGE 99

VIII
ONLY GENTLEMEN GUN QUAIL
PAGE 111

DEDICATION

This book is dedicated to the members of
Ducks Unlimited, whose untiring efforts
assure a bright future for North America's
waterfowl, and to the memory of
Harold Marsh Henshaw, IV, (1961-1978) a young
sportsman and active member of that organization.

EDITOR'S NOTE: Many of the line drawings used in this book are taken from Mr. Maass' working drawings which he used to create the paintings.

FOREWORD

This book is the blending of the outstanding talents of two very remarkable men, one an artist the other a writer. It is elegant evidence that the American outdoor painting and writing tradition is alive and thriving—and has attained a new level of excellence in this unique collaboration between David Maass' extraordinary painting and Gene Hill's particularly effective prose.

I have known Gene Hill for about twenty years. I've known David Maass through his paintings for nearly the same length of time. Both men have said, one through words the other through his pictures, what I believe to be the essence of the outdoor experience. Each man constantly strives to improve to search out the perfection that eludes us all, to uncover previously undiscovered secrets and insights in wildlife and our experiences with it.

David Maass paints the birds he knows and loves best—waterfowl and upland birds. He considers himself a "landscape artist who puts wildlife into a painting" and, as such, lends an important, almost painstaking authentic detail to his paintings. The clear tranquil scenes which he creates with an uncompromising use of rich colors and sharp detail have won critical acclaim throughout the country and have made David Maass the most popular wildlife artist in America today.

Gene Hill writes for the classic "Everyman" and every man finds something in his writing that is personally meaningful. I have shared some of the best experiences of the hunting and fishing world with Gene, but it still never ceases to bring a small touch of wonder to me when I read his work. He saw something in a little thing—a broken dog lead or an empty shotgun shell—the rest of us missed. And he told us about it as only he can do and we knew something more about what happened and about ourselves, too. I doubt that there is another living outdoor writer who commands the respect and affection that Gene has among his followers who must rank in the hundred of thousands at this time.

I commend this book to your attention without reservation. There will be few like it to come your way, so treasure your moments with its prose and paintings. As with most good things in life, the time will be too short.

Jim Rikhoff

June 19, 1978
Speakeasy Hill
Highbridge, New Jersey

THE GAME OF GROUSE

Misty Morning—Ruffed Grouse

It wasn't the shooting of grouse, or even the hunting of it, that first created the appeal for the bird that later would grow into a small passion. What attracted me, even as a small boy, was the *ethic* of grouse hunting. The introduction to this ethic was given to me in the person, and his trappings, of the first real grouse hunter I ever saw.

His name is not important. Nor is the fact (which I know now) that he was known to be a confirmed loafer who lived on his wife's income—and a man who on occasion drank a bit more than was socially necessary. What is important here is the fact that he was elegant; he had style. He even had a "shooting car." I can clearly remember the times I used to see him drive by on the dirt road that led past the farm. The wood body of his Model A Ford station wagon framed the faces of two or three English setters, in other years an Irish, and I seem to recall one sad-faced Gordon, his chin bouncing uncomfortably on the window frame as the stiff-sprung Ford caromed over the "thank-you-ma'ams."

Sometimes he would park out back by our old orchard, and I would stand unseen, behind the October-copper leaves of a blackberry bramble, and watch. He almost always wore a tie, an old tweed jacket, and breeches with high leather boots. A felt hat

Over the Pond—Ruffed Grouse

framed his lean and handsome face, and he would often make some small ceremony of lighting his pipe before extracting his Parker from its saddle leather case. One dog was then summoned from the wagon, and as they walked out of sight, I would hear the sweet click of the breech closing and often be able to distinguish the lingering fragrance of tobacco in the apple-scented air.

My Partridge Man passed away before I became of gunning age so I never even got to do more than wave (unseen, for all I know) to him from along the road during gunning season, but somehow, even then, bib-overalled and all as I was—I understood him. And, back in my mind, the picture of what a partridge hunter should look like helped me understand what a partridge hunter is... and why he is the way he is.

A partridge hunter is deeply into the pursuit of something more than a pound of bird. He is involved in the pleasure he gets out of walking around with a graceful 20-gauge or the like. He is much taken with the idea of days afield in the companionship of similar-minded friends. He is much pleased with clucking to a tricolor setter with a merry gait or a lemon-and-white Brittany with smiling eyes. And last, but not really—he enjoys missing something that seems to be a brown-flecked sound that, more often than not, scares him half to death. And should he, by an action he cannot explain or commonly duplicate, manage to take a grouse in full flight, he is somewhat saddened by the unfairness of the bird he has coveted from this special fox-grape cluster flying heedlessly into an ounce of his randomly thrown 8's.

The Grouse Hunter is not a hunter. The grouse is not a real bird. The man is a pipe-smoking, dog-loving, walnut-stock-coveting mystic. The grouse is a will-o-the-wisp, an ephemeral creature, a laurel-hidden siren. One must hide, and the other must seek.

And the game is played according to the rules—according to the *ethic*. The real grouse hunter wants to *hunt* grouse—not *shoot* them, at least not shoot any more than the three or six a season that result from playing the game.

The grouse himself exists to be studied by a variety of ornithologists, biologists, and varied cycle-watchers. He exists in order that beautifully illustrated books may be written about him. He is a creation that justifies the supporting of a kennelful of bird dogs for ten months a year so that the grouse hunter can hunt weekends for two months. The grouse *is* so we can listen to his drumming, count his chicks, and keep a worried eye on the berries that he likes to eat. The grouse looks the way he does so that he will grace the

Thundering Out
RUFFED GROUSE

engraving on slim-barreled, straight-hand, Circassian-stocked, improved-cylinder and modified shotguns with two-syllable names and price tags with a lot of zeros on them.

Where the ruffed grouse is hunted with passion, no living thing is really wilder. Unlike almost any other bird or beast, he cannot be tamed, domesticated or catered to. Man has not been able to get his hands on this bird, so to speak; and, as a result, he is one of the few pure things we have left in an environment that is otherwise carrying all sorts of crossbred, artificially-inseminated, transplanted, and laboratory-raised creatures. He has managed to survive fire, plague, do-gooders, land-development barons, and, so far, even the Corps of Army Engineers have not been able to drain him dry, flood him out, or turn all of his nooks and crannies into public recreation parking lots.

The Grouse Hunter today seems to have more natural enemies than the grouse, but, bless him, he too is holding on. And, I note happily, he is even allowed to breed, as I see an occasional young Grouse Hunter in the coverts every fall. The Grouse Hunter spends his time in what behavioral scientists call the Nirvana stage. His wife often calls it something else, but it is essentially the same thing: A great deal of productive time (time spent by others doing useful things like earning a living, taking the children to

Autumn Day—Ruffed Grouse

points of educational interest . . . etc., etc.) is spent around the problems of outwitting a small feathered creature with an IQ about the same as a yellow perch.

The Grouse Hunter's yearly calendar might read more or less like this:

January: Attend local meeting of Venerable Grouse Hunters to discuss the crafty methods used by the members who took a total of nine grouse last season.

February: Start looking at advertisements for a new puppy from "proven grouse blood that does it all!" to fool with.

March: Reread Burton Spiller's grouse books for the fortieth time. Ditto, Foster's grouse book, Knight's grouse book, et al.

April: Take grouse gun, very carefully, to skeet club to sharpen eye.

May: Take grouse gun to gunsmith to have the choke in right barrel opened up 2/1000 of an inch.

June: Take six-month-old puppy to secret dog trainer that is known only to a thousand other grouse hunters. Trainer reputed (falsely) to work only with grouse dogs.

July: Take family on so-called vacation trip to areas reputed to have superb grouse cover. Area mapped. Chicks counted. Local liquor laws and prices examined.

August: Order new type of vest from Eddie Bauer catalog. New type of upland coat from Orvis. New boots from L.L. Bean. New collars, leashes, whistles, etc., etc.

September: Get puppy back from trainer. Spend enough time in field with him to undo all the training.

October: Hunt grouse. Twenty-two fair shots at game. Two birds. Have first bird mounted because puppy flushed it.

November: Take long, expensive hunting trip to sit in cabin and play gin rummy, discuss choke boring and watch snow or rain.

December: Treat self to another new Remington, Ithaca, Browning, Winchester, Webley, Savage or something similar for Christmas on basis of working so hard. Send grouse Xmas cards. Get grouse Xmas cards. Get grouse print from son. Grouse highball glasses from wife. New grouse book from

Back County—Ruffs
RUFFED GROUSE

daughter. A good Christmas. Look forward to coming January meeting with Venerables.

The annual calendar of the grouse would be somewhat different, but the Grouse Hunter has come to believe that, except for the brief time spent in the business of drumming, bragging and dancing, and getting the chicks set up on their own wings, the grouse is constantly scheming and plotting.

How else can it happen that time after time a certain patch of sumac and briers will contain a grouse that never does the same thing twice over a period of fifty flushes in two seasons? No matter how the trap is set, it forever comes up empty. The ultimate scorn that I ever received at the hands (wings?) of this puzzling bird was after walking up behind my setter, locked in one of the very few classic points she ever made. I saw the grouse sitting, head upright and alert and staring first at the dog and then at me.

Was I ever ready! I shuffled my feet and braced for the grenade-like flush. The bird cocked her head and continued to stare at us. The dog backed off a step or two and looked at me, as if shrugging her shoulders. The bird, acting as bored and nonchalant as a shoplifter, very simply just walked away and eventually disappeared in the brush, leaving the magazine-cover scene of man-and-dog doing-it-all just-right-in-October, with

Hasty Departure—Ruffed Grouse

Ridge Line—Ruffed Grouse

me standing there feeling completely ridiculous.

I'm convinced that grouse like grouse dogs. The presence of a grouse dog further insures against the Grouse Hunter ever getting a fair shot. A good definition of a grouse dog is any kind of a dog that will be seen in the company of a grouse hunter. The only grouse most grouse dogs ever see close-up are in illustrations in expensive books. I know all about the pictures of guys reaching down to take the bird from the mouth of their dog. I've got a couple of those myself, but I don't expect to be admitted to heaven on that basis, nor would I even like to stand up on oath and testify on all the circumstances involved.

Grouse dogs are never where they should be, and rarely where their human companion thinks they are. And they are never near grouse—except by accident. The few times I was really vindictive and for one reason or another really wanted to bag a bird or so, I used my kid brother—who, while not as stylish as a Llewellin setter or as sleek as a pointer, would at least do as he was told, and succeeded in flushing quite a few birds in the right direction. After all, the heavily-hunted grouse has come to learn how harmless a creature the average human being is (that's precisely my brother—

harmless and average). The hunter who *has* to have tail fans soon learns that grouse can be driven like deer and goes at his hunting with that knowledge. He might take a dog along for local color, but he leaves him in the car or tied to the brass rail at Mario's Tavern for a couple of hours, if he's serious about roast grouse for Sunday dinner.

Of course, I know that some decent grouse dogs must exist somewhere outside the imagination of fiction writers, but I suspect more good bird dogs are whelped in front of log fires from jars of Jack Daniels than anyplace else in the world. I say that not to discredit the dogs, but to do honor to the grouse. At various times, the bird has to watch out for the evil intent of owls, cats, foxes, hawks, weasels, and skunks, while trying to scratch out a living. He is ready for "come what may"—the average dog, I'm sorry to say, is not.

On my littered desk is a small bell, the ordinary little tinkler you might find on any bird dog's collar. I ring it now and then, when no one else is listening, and it still sounds the way it used to when my first setter carried it around her swan-white neck. There was a river bottom that we especially liked to hunt. Not because it was

Forest Vigil
RUFFED GROUSE

birdy—and it wasn't—but because it was beautiful. The way down to the bottom was through a fragrant stand of tall white pines that gave way to some wild rhododendron and then some kind of fern. I used to stand there and listen to the little bell solo against the running of the water and try to memorize the sounds and smells so I could summon them up in other places at other times, and they would comfort me.

And every so often, right where the rhododendrons started, a grouse would flight to give me another sight and sound to store away.

Every partridge hunter should have an end-of-the-day covert—a cool place for himself to sit and listen, and a spot for a drink and a swim for the dog. It's a nice quiet place to dress a bird, if you have one, and if not—why, no matter at all. You can sit a minute or two and sort things out, watch a worry or so wash away in the stream, and discover that the end of one hunt is the beginning of another.

No one will fault you if you make the harmless wish that you could follow the tinkle of this dog's bell through a lifetime of grouse covers, and when it was all done, you both could rest forever by this riverbank, smelling the pines and the ferns.

A BACKYARD HUDSON'S BAY

Startled Takeoff
WOOD DUCKS

We called it a pondhole—which meant it was too small to be a pond and too big to be a hole. If memory serves, and I'm not at all sure it does, the place was about a hundred and fifty yards in diameter, ringed by pin oaks and silver maples up high and hazel and wild blackberries down low ... but just on three sides. I built my blind, in some defiance of knowing better, on the relatively open side, because it backed up against a cliff of sorts that was once used by Indians as a source of stone for arrowheads and knives.

I always found comfort in knowing (or at least hoping) that some Algonquin or Delaware or Lenape had crouched just where I crouched, anxiously waiting for some duck to swim within the very questionable lethality of me and my shotgun.

Buried a little ways back in the woods, I found a long-dry well, the remnants of a log cabin, and a pile of rocks that I guessed had been destined for a fireplace and chimney. So, if I exhausted my imagination regarding the Indians and their goings on, I could mull over the variety of romantic and tragic stories that might be told about the mouldering logs and the cairn of fieldstones.

As you can see, I liked this spot for a number of reasons, aside from its use as

Autumn Marsh — Mallards

Leveling Off
PINTAILS

picnic grounds for blacks and pintails and an occasional teal or mallard. I had a choice of paths to and from my pondhole and carefully alternated them in the fear that some wandering rabbit hunter might see a too-worn trail and follow it to my private preserve.

I had hidden in a pint canning jar a cheap corncob pipe and a nickel paper of a very vile tobacco called George Washington—advertised, as I recall, as being the ideal choice for rolling cigarettes, pipes or chewing; I doubt if it was good for any of these, and I marvel that I continued to smoke in spite of its fearful fumes, my mother's hatred of the habit, and the expense to my non-existent budget. But, somehow, the idea of sitting there, puffing tentative practice smoke rings until my tongue blistered, added the final touch to my vision of myself as a would-be mountain man; and, by just closing my eyes, I could be dressed in buckskin, fringed, of course, and palavering in pretty good fashion, complete with the two or three gestures of "finger talk" I had picked up in my brief encounter with the Boy Scouts.

In those days you could buy at any good country general store a pair of what was known as "over-the-knee" boots. How far over depended on how tall you were, but they

Western Marsh—Pintails

The River Flats—Pintails

Twisting Through—Blue-Winged Teal

Misty Morning — Mallards

were never over enough for wading in anything more than a rivulet. Any retrieving chores in my wind-sheltered pothole necessitated going in over the tops; why I didn't just take the boots off and wade wet escapes me now, but I know I never did. No doubt, getting wet and a little bit cold only enhanced the mood of wilderness and adventure—part and parcel of being out on your own, surviving against the elements—with home and a glowing wood-burning kitchen stove a brisk hour's walk away, just the right distance in the dark to have its owl-calling moments of chilling thrills before the yellow lights of the farmhouse appeared with their promise of warmth and security.

My pondhole delivered the occasional duck before freezing over early in November, and now and then a gray squirrel or rabbit, but that was the small end of its purpose. To a yearling farm boy with an imagination that bordered on runaway, it served magnificently as a frontier: at times an ocean, more often an unnamed mountain bivouac, or the headwaters of a wilderness river. It lent credence, in its way, to the visions of Hudson's Bay, the Rocky Mountains, and eager comparisons with the lives of Carson and Boone, Lewis and Clark, Bridger and Green.

On the Move
GREEN-WINGED TEAL

[32]

Graceful Descent
BALDPATES

River's Edge—Mallards

Peaceful Pair
MALLARDS

My ducks were messengers from places unknown and truly wild, passing through from what I believed to be moose and caribou country to equally believed tropics filled with anacondas and bushmasters—how I wished then, and still do, that I could see for myself the lands they saw and lived in. And their just being there—those pintails and blacks—in front of my oak and hazel and cedar blind created a belief in things I could only dream about—their wings whispered that all these things were real and true; that they had seen and known places and creatures that would beggar my wildest dreams.

My visions of exploring these wondrous tracts never failed to include the company of what was the most longed-for thing in my life—an exact duplicate of my father's gun (forbidden to me then, of course), that most exquisite piece of machinery known as a Winchester model 97 hammer pump. With this in hand, I would be fearless, unconquerable, and completely self-sufficient... anywhere. I'd sneak it out and shuck it when no one was around and marvel at how perfect it sounded as the various rods and slides drew a shell from the magazine up into the chamber, the bolt slid the hammer back as slick as anything, and it all closed with consummate authority and sat poised to strike with a power that to me was akin to lightning. Then I would work it empty again, ease the hammer back to half, the way Pop left it, wipe it off, and place it back in the closet exactly where it always sat.

Before I was big enough to handle it, Pop traded the 97 for another pump he never liked as well. And then we moved. The fact that the pondhole and the pump are gone are indisputable. But I still have my pintails and the occasional black... and, now and then, have gone where, no doubt, some Indian has walked before. The dreams have

Misty Morning—Wood Ducks

1977 Minnesota Duck Stamp Design
MALLARDS

Stopover
BLACK DUCKS

1974-75 Federal Duck Stamp Design
WOOD DUCKS

shrunk somewhat and the night-calling owls bring another kind of chilling thought...a moment beyond the help of even Pop's old model 97. But the hushing sound of wings can still evoke that timeless magic, and, as I watch them slant above my hiding place, I still wonder, as always, what it was they saw yesterday and what they will see tomorrow.

REFLECTIONS ON THE BAY

On the Move—Canvasbacks

When you think of divers, think big water—those great American bays, some adorned with their Indian names; others re-christened with a thought of home to make this foreign land at least a little bit like England. All the places have that right ring to the duck hunter's ear. I especially like the sounds of Susquehanna and Chesapeake; I like the old-time pictures they bring to mind: the black and white studies of pipe-smoking baymen; the long-porched rich men's gunning clubs; the stilted marsh shacks with their windward chimneys; the young sports, derby-hatted and nonchalant, with their 10 bores in one hand and a string of birds stretched out to frame them.

It was down here that the skills of the drawknife and rasp brought out the art of the decoy about as much as anyplace. None of them would have ever admitted it, but they gunned for market more for the gunning than the lean profit—which was, more often than not, dribbled back into shells and boats and guns—probably just the way they really wanted it. They were the master practitioners of sink boxes, batteries, scull-oared bushwhackers, punts, pungies, skiffs, sneakers, and almost anything else that would float a man or two out and hopefully back.

Imagine a bay with over five thousand miles of shoreline—a bay where only the Lord and the watermen knew, or prayed they did, the ins and outs of countless creeks, guts, rivers, tidal runs, and channels, and the whereabouts of the permanent and occasional islands. Imagine a time when the only "small craft warnings" were in your head and your heart, and, if you were wrong, it was a long walk back—or worse. But when the wind was right with the promise of worsening weather, and the night was alive with the soft brush of wings and the burring calls of cans, redheads, and bluebills, they'd itch and get ready.

Getting ready then was a little different than it is for us today. There were the boats to be seen to, the rigs of three or four hundred decoys had to be right, and fresh shells had to be loaded and old ones pulled out from under the stove, where they'd been put to dry.

Some went out by trustworthy horse and buggy, others by less trustworthy model T's, to creekside brush blinds and the like. Others sailed, or poled, or rowed in the pitch

Out of the North
LESSER SCAUP

dark with the only markers in their memory and sixth sense navigation. Some who favored the punt guns, were already there, hand-paddling down a shaft of moonlight or weaving through the white death of ice floes. They had their bellies to the cold top of the Chesapeake, steering a half-pound of shot in a "big one" that lay tied down with rope and heeled-up on a thatch of marsh hay or seaweed against the stern-cracking recoil. In the front of the boat was a coal oil gunning lamp, its flickering yellow light backed by some sort of reflector. Up in the front of their mind was canvasbacks, redheads or bluebills, backed by some sort of prayers against fog, offshore wind, and a swamping chop.

If you were a market gunner in a serious way, you probably worked with a helper in a pick-up boat—someone who marked and retrieved the bag, while you did the best you could with a pair of guns to make each shot count—and the knotting flight of the divers often gave you the chance to bring down two or even three with each barrel. And later, with the coming of the semi-automatics, you'd no doubt add an extension to the magazine to give you an extra six or eight shots. Bags of over a hundred ducks a day weren't uncommon, and a few gunners were so highly skilled that they could get by with just the shooting end of the job—no rowing, no picking up decoys.

By common agreement the market gunners usually restricted their shooting to three days a week—Monday, Wednesday, and Friday—but the "season" ran from September until March, and the toll they took was immense. The era of the market shooter ended in 1918. And in the early thirties a rather strict, for then, system of Federal laws was formulated, including the forbidding of live decoys. But I, for one, find it not too difficult to ease the blame from the oldtimers. And, in truth, the progress of civilization had about as much to do with the diminishing waterfowl as anything.

Had I lived along the Chesapeake in those days at the turn of the century, I know where I would have been when the flights began drifting down from the north. Assuming that my skills as a wing shot would be what they are now, I'd have been one of the youngsters who looked at the "professional" with awe and worship, and no doubt you could have found me hanging around the carvers and the guns and the pick-up men trying to glean what I could of their skills, imitating their mannerisms, using their figures of speech, and hoping against hope that some day they'd ask me to come along.

But I'm dead sure that I'd have arranged some sort of gunning for myself. How I'd love to have owned a set of live callers and the other trappings that went with being a serious ducker: a decoy rig, some sort of skiff, and a 32-inch ten or twelve gauge side-by-side; then at least I might start to look the part—if you were inclined to be charitable.

I think that one of the reasons duck hunting has such an immense appeal to us is that nothing else really demands such a combination of skills if you go at it at all seriously. Back in the old days, one of the basic codes was: If you want it done right, do it yourself. Of course, this was backed up pretty heavily by the fact that if you couldn't do it, it wasn't likely to get done at all. So, of necessity and pride, as many as could do so carved their own decoys—and there weren't too many watermen who weren't more than handy with their daily tools. (Think of how many of the classic carvers called themselves Captain . . . and of the others that could have.)

They knew the weather, and from having spent so much of their lives out there where everything happened where they could see it, their predictions on bird habits were not our modern-day wishful thinking. And after a few seasons of gunning six or

Winter Wings
BUFFLEHEADS

[49]

Red Head Bay

Breaking In—Bluebills
LESSER SCAUP

seven (or more) months a year, they got to be pretty handy with a shotgun. Now, add to that the skills of proper blind construction, dog training for those who wanted that sort of helper, some others who liked to call, those who trained live decoys—and it turns out that your really accomplished waterfowler was a man of many parts.

So here we have that mythical set of circumstances that for once actually happened and went beyond history into legend. We have the Susquehanna Flats prolific with wild celery, we have every conceivable type of water and land and food combination that the waterfowl needed and wanted. We have, consequently, flights of birds that will never again exist except in print, memory, and folklore. And we have the right kind of men with the right skills at the right time and place. Not that we need too much more to make this scene beyond any reproach, but we would be remiss to ignore another factor. Among all the divers, among all the other ducks as well, we have the fact that the canvasback has a singular destiny: the table!

In the hands of even the nervous, anxious, unsure bride (given that she could tell time and temperature) the canvasback would provide a supper that was sure to provoke compliments, or at least not be criticized, depending on the character of the groom. In the hands of a decent chef, of which this country has more than its share—many no doubt attracted by the local bounty that included terrapin, several varieties of oysters, upland birds, shore birds, and a nearly endless choice of fish—the canvasback rightfully took its place at the very pinnacle of dining.

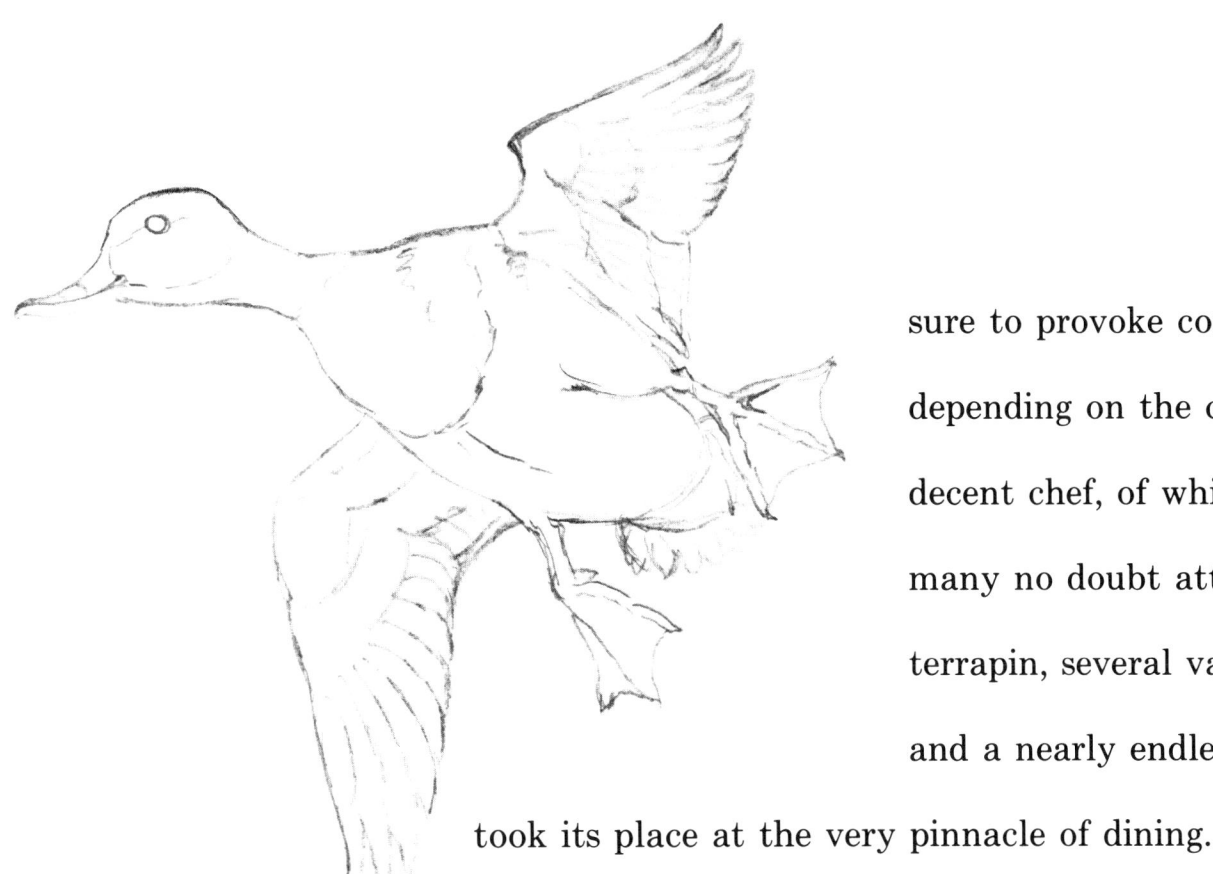

In those days when a man's girth was symbolic of his hold on life's better things, the feats at dinner were equal to Roman times. After an appetite-honing portion of the local rye whiskey, a gentleman could look forward to terrapin or snapper soup and a brace or so of woodcock, snipe, curlew, or the like. Next came a respite with several dozen oysters and a palate-cleansing selection of fish; and then, when he had his gastric system properly warmed-up, the platters of canvasback would arrive. We must respectfully remember that, along with his tantalizing nibbling, he would be taking a light port wine or dry sherry, Bordeaux or claret, one or more white wines, or perhaps a bottle of champagne; and, unquestionably, he would end the gentle repast with cognac, brandy, or something on the order of a Chateau Yquem to give balance to a variety of cheeses, pies, trifles, and a selection of more delicate pastries.

For those of you who ever wondered why the era of the market gunner lasted as long as it did, I refer you to the menus of the more noted hotels of our major cities and ask that you recall pictures you have seen of the likes of Diamond Jim Brady, Grover Cleveland, and William Howard Taft.

Wherever and whenever the law and good fortune allow me the privilege of taking a canvasback, visions of white linen, glittering candelabra, wine decanters of cut crystal, and a variety of elegantly-shaped glasses come to my mind. I can see myself, starched shirt, wing-collar and all, resting one foot upon a red velvet-covered gout stool, while watching the long ash grow from my hand-rolled Havana cigar. And, somewhat sadly, knowing that this is never to be, I gather my feathered treasure, reduce all my dreamy

Sweeping the Narrows—Canvasbacks

visions by ninety percent, and sit there idly plucking myself back to reality.

Our hammer side-by-sides have become pump guns and now-and-then automatics. The three-hundred-bird cedar rigs have been replaced by a dozen or so plastic replicas bobbing stiffly in front of a makeshift blind. The pick-up man nuzzles her half-trained head into my coat pocket, sniffing the remnants of an undersized and overpriced chocolate bar. A freshening northeast breeze carries the sound of a small flock banking and turning into the wind, and I instinctively grab the dog's collar and look as carefully as I can, trying to identify the birds, trying to remember the points they carry by Federal law, and watch, almost in tears, as a dozen redheads and cans flop noisily amidst my decoys. I wait a few minutes, idly dreaming, and send Josephine out to flush them—then sit back again, hoping something better will come along. But it can't—it doesn't exist.

VOICES FROM WOODCOCK COUNTRY

Tricky Target
WOODCOCK

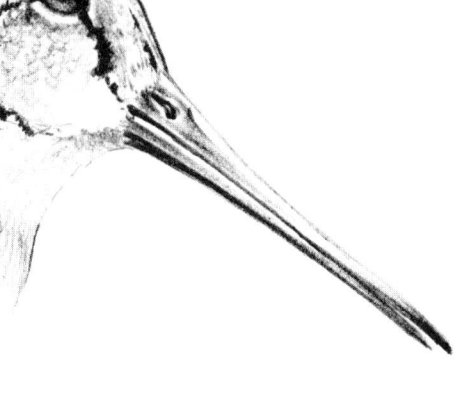

Although I didn't know it at the time, the first good woodcock dog I ever saw was an orange Belton setter about the size of a young heifer. His owner was one of those florid-faced men who looked as though he had slept in the bow tie he was wearing. He had the build of a butcher and the soft, low voice of a choir master. He spoke to his dog in tones that carried affection, trust and complete understanding. This was the sort of companionship that you knew had many years of close living and working together behind it. I could barely imagine the man driving or walking anywhere without the big setter at his side.

They had devised a curious and thoroughly effective method of hunting the bottom covers. The cap-and-bow-tie would find a spot to his liking and stand still. The dog would then amble out about 40 or 50 yards and begin a slow series of circles that either ended up in a point (not really a point, but more of a standing-still and looking at where the bird sat) or back with his owner. The hunter would then walk on to another likely spot, and the dog would begin his circling back all over again.

He noticed my watching him one afternoon, and when he called me over, I broke open my single-shot 20-gauge, adjusted the couple of rabbits I had in my sack, and joined him. "That's Jack," he said, nodding toward the setter, who looked away as if he were ashamed to be seen so close to a cottontail brush jumper. "You can hunt with me if you'd like to try a few woodcock, and if Jack pushes out a rabbit, why, just go ahead and shoot it. He won't pay any attention."

We walked awhile together, silent, until he found a spot to his liking. "Stand over there," he said, pointing to a scrub birch clump. "If a bird gets up, or Jack goes on point, you get the first shot, okay?" I nodded, and Jack began his curious corkscrewing through the woods, looking over at me now and then, as if to confirm his opinion that he was working for what was obviously the world's worst wingshot. Jack had me pegged about right. The full-choked single 20 was a lightning strike on a sitting rabbit, but I'd wasted enough heavy 6's on various birds to know that I was not born to shake the throne of Fred Kimble. I dreaded both the flushed bird and the pointed one, and missed a chance at each. I told the man that I'd rather watch, and, in the next hour, I saw him take four birds with four right barrels of his side-by-side L. C. Smith.

When we came out of the brook bottom, his car was there by the edge of the road. I thanked him and told him I hoped we'd meet again, but declined his offer of a ride, on

Misty Morning—Woodcock

the chance of picking up another rabbit or two on the walk home. "Is your mother a good cook?" he asked. She wasn't, but I didn't know that then, so I said yes. He reached around inside his hunting coat, and, after smoothing each one, dropped the four birds in my rabbit sack. I started to protest, but he stopped me short by saying, "Jack and I get our share. Just remember where you see some when you're hunting, and next time we meet you can take *me* along."

Country people, back then, didn't ply each other with a lot of questions, so I never learned his name, nor he mine. I assume now, looking back, that we had hit the last part of the flight, and we never again met in the woods, nor did I ever see his roadster parked along any of the roads I walked. But we did hunt together, in my imagination, many a time after. Sitting in the oak and hickory watching for squirrels, I could see myself with a bird dog of my own and an identical L. C. Smith, leading the old hunter to a secret alder cover teeming with woodcock. There I would distinguish myself by never having to dirty the left barrel. A lot of time has gone by, but it hasn't diminished this dream one whit—nor has any of it come true.

The half-mystery of my first meeting with a woodcock hunter, and the even greater mystery of the bird itself, lit a fire that has consumed me ever since. It has also consumed countless days of meandering bottom covers peppered with birches or silvered with popple. It has consumed countless days of fooling with a variety of shotguns in the endless (I'm sure) search for the precisely right combination of weight, balance, barrel length and choke. And it has consumed countless days of fooling with various bird dogs in another endless search for the precise amounts of bidability, range, nose and companionship. I count those times among my most treasured hours.

The best woodcock covers are often not the kind you'll see in a painting. Nor are they to be analyzed by soil type, cover, sun or shade. I have found woodcock in such unlikely places as in the midst of ideal quail cover in northeast Texas; in high, rock-strewn ledges where the scrawny evergreens send out root tendrils in the moss searching for soil; and even along the edge of my driveway. The true woodcock gunner finds himself drawn to what suits his nature—not necessarily the ideal. My instincts lead me to where I can hear the swamp-edge soil sucking lightly at my leather-topped rubber boots. I enjoy the possibility of discovering a hidden spring, a trickle of brook packed with watercress, and, of course, the telltale little splashes of whitewash that indicate visitors. I like being down out of the wind with the pungent smells of May apples, skunk cabbage and hemlock. I like the feeling of constant change you get in the low country—as against the semi-permanence of the wind-ridden high ridges that seem unalterable.

My setters like the low country, too. One long-ago, lovely, orange-ticked white ghost named Jag delighted in flinging herself in the cool mud and coming out looking like a troll. If there aren't any woodcock, there are almost always frogs, snakes, or the occasional muskrat to worry up. There is always something.

There are those gunners who say that the actual shooting of a woodcock is anticlimactic, claiming that the birds offer no challenge to the expert shot. In reply, I use a common synonym for a byproduct of cattle raising. I would like to take some of these so-called experts to one of my favorite bottom covers. I defy them to take a limit of four birds with sixteen shells. I further defy them to throw their hat on the ground and have it hit, for the place to which I would take them is what you might call a thicket—if the word thicket still carries the strength I attribute to it. Here you will hear woodcock in numbers; you will see several; but you'll be able to swing on very few. And I love it. This is hunting; this is getting down to what it's all about. This is

Autumn Birch—Woodcock

coming home proud that you took a couple of birds from a pocket-dark, shadow-ridden, fight-your-way-through alder cover. This is 24-inch-barrel, no-choke, shoot-from-the-hip cover. This is where your soft-footed setter sounds like a moose as she climbs over and through stuff that you can't. This is where you discover that woodcock don't hold like all the books tell you, where birds fly like silent puffs of smoke. This is where it really is!

There are famous woodcock covers where you can go out and take a limit between a late breakfast and lunch, but I don't like them. These are usually not feeding covers, but the resting ones that birds use after a long and arduous flight. You're pushing out birds that are tired, if not exhausted. This is not hunting, and I want no part of it. Neither do your fine Michigan sportsmen, or your classic New England gunners, or those lucky enough to spend October in New Brunswick. They love this bird above all and believe in a fair chase. They know the times and places where they can feel proud to take a bird or two for a companion piece to a sturdy red wine. They want to earn it the hard way, because woodcock deserve no less.

The oldtime woodcock hunters that I knew liked most to hunt alone. They carted tall, long-headed Gordon or English setters with a slow, thorough pace. There was no hint of hurry, no mention of covering so many miles, no bragging about bags. They'd come back and sit in the country store and tell you as much about what was going on in the woods as they would about the hunt itself—often more. They were quiet men who, I believe, found a reward in an afternoon with a dog and their old 20-bore Parkers that was more personal and fulfilling than many of us, time-ridden and pushed by inner demands, can ever feel today. They mussed with puppies, and felt more comfortable around horses than they did with cars. They talked about old orchards that still bore Pound Sweets; about bee trees, seeing trout, and where Indian moccasin grew. They remembered the name of everyone else's dogs and chatted about them with enthusiasm and honest affection.

In fact, they would talk at length about almost anything—except exactly where they had been gunning. You'd ask Marvin or Ely where they thought some birds might be and one would say, "Well, you might find a couple up around back of Culver's Lake," thereby loosely directing you to an area of about fifteen square miles. Only a kid would have had the naivete to even ask. The other oldtimers wouldn't have wasted their hard-cider breath, knowing the answer would bear only the haziest relation to the facts

Resting Wings
WOODCOCK

of the matter. Even back then there were the jokes about taking you out sometime "only I'd have to blindfold both you and Old Jack."

I'd see these local legends now and then at the store. They'd buy a box of shells for sixty cents, or, if times were hard, a half a dozen or so single shells for three cents apiece. A box of crackers and a good wedge of rat cheese was a dime. For the dog there'd be some home-made cornbread in the car. If it was cider-making time, fifteen cents would fill a gallon jug (no charge for the cooling damp feed sack to wrap it in). To me, more or less gunless and dogless, they were giants with skills and knowledge beyond my personal hope. How could I ever be like them? Nothing in my foreseeable future promised an English or a Gordon. The Bakers and LeFevers, the Remingtons and Parkers, the Smiths and Foxes that could be seen, from a distance, at the hardware store—they were as remote to me as ever getting my chores done. The leggings and the high-laced leather boots were the uniforms of generals seen through the eyes of a career private.

Yet, I knew that someday my turn would come. What I did not suspect was that it would be in another, less glamorous, time. I felt a great loss, driving back through this country with my English setter and my 16-gauge L. C. Smith, knowing that the companions I so desperately wanted to talk with were no longer around. Nor was the store with its 10-cent cheese and crackers, its 60-cent shells and its cider mill, with the tin cup and full bucket for the visitor to sample while he waited for a fresh pressing. The twisting dirt roads that had held such adventure and promise were either oiled or paved. All that was left were some of the woodcock covers, and those I mostly had to myself. Yes, I took my pleasures in them—but how I longed for a country store that welcomed your dog or for an oldtimer to swing and admire my L.C. Smith the way I had so often seen them do with each other's guns. How I wished for the questions about where it was that Little Ben and I had done so well—and to have been able to rock back in my chair, fuss with my pipe, and describe an area that was close, but not too close, while a farm boy scratched Ben's ears and looked at me with wonder and envy.

What I wouldn't give to have heard as I left the store that priceless sentence that I had so often heard about Marvin or Ely: *"That Hilly there, him and that Ben dog is about as good a pair as you'll find anywhere when it comes to woodcock."* I do hear it now and then, but like so much of what we yearn for, it is only a man hearing voices in his imagination from a time that he lives in all alone.

TWO's, FOUR's and XXL's

Gliding In

CANADA GEESE

I say to you that I can tell a serious goose hunter from a serious duck hunter, and you say I'm crazy. Maybe so, maybe not. Serious goose hunters tend to look like geese. That is to say, while your serious duck hunter tends to be average in girth and general heft, your serious goose hunter tends to be more so, to be polite.

I think this is pure "natural selection," as our anthropologist friends would say. The goose hunter has to be powerful. Take the average load of gear that he so enjoys carrying around: His several calls range from large to huge. (One goose gunner I know favors calls that look like flutes or piccolos and carries several.) The real giveaway, aside from his gun, which we'll touch on in a minute, is the lunch pail. Your average duck hunter, who is built along the spare lines of a dentist, will make do with an ordinary salami and swiss cheese, maybe a peanut butter and grape jelly (if he doesn't intend to do much calling), a banana or apple (which he never eats, but always carries since his mother started him out with those traditions in the second grade), and a pint thermos of coffee with cream and three sugars. Thus, we have a basic and rather unimaginative cuisine, but common, and only slightly below the level of a guide's lunch, which substitutes cookies for the fruit and always includes an ancient green-yolked boiled egg, which is traditionally fed to the retriever—sometimes shelled, sometimes not, depending on the quality of the dog.

The goose hunter needs heartier fare. Underneath the XXL camouflage parka is a boy without straight lines—a figure that would do credit to a Milanese basso-buffo. The goose hunter is a man constructed along the heroic lines of a Viking—fond of, and with access to, free beer. He spurns the lunch pail as fitting only for teen-age girls. His snack goes to the blind in a wood firkin or a sturdy split-cane basket.

The goose hunter doesn't eat—he dines. Almost certainly there will be a paté, or sardines to stimulate the gastric juices. After the antipasto, he will embrace half a cold chicken, sliced tongue, and cold roast beef with horseradish, topped off with seedless grapes, cheese and coconut layer cake washed down with black coffee carrying an ounce or so of dark rum or brandy. Then, secure in the knowledge that geese will not demand his attention during the civilized ritual of early afternoon, he will nap.

A man hunting ducks cannot so indulge himself, since the duck is as unpredictable as a bride—doing strange things without any reason, calculated to upset the plans of the man involved. Duck hunters are nervous of temperament anyway, as would anyone be

Homeward Bound
SNOW GEESE

who has to cope with the brashness of broadbills, the wariness of blacks, the nitwittery of teal, and still be alert enough not to draw down on such intruders as coot, shovellers or any of several species of fish-eaters.

But a gentleman setting out to deal with the majestic Canada can do so without the aid of antacids and can spare himself the need of being forever on the visual *qui vive*. When geese are coming around, they are sports enough to announce it. A man has time to put his coffee cup on the shelf of the blind, adjust his hat, take off the safety, remember that he has to lead oncomers by three and a half feet and crossing shots by five or six and then stand up and do neither—that not being the fault of the goose, but part of the ritual of the serious goose hunter.

Most of the goose hunter's equipage is as specialized as his sport—and as much out of necessity as inclination. Years ago, the goose hunter absolutely knew that he would spend the day in the blind with his body reaching a near-fatal low temperature. No matter how calculated the layers of wool over the layers of hunter (laid down carefully by seconds and thirds of mashed potatoes and gravy), he was in for it heavily when it came to chills and frostbite. Few, if any, waterproof garments even remotely repelled a light drizzle for more than fifteen minutes. His feet, unless they were encased in felt boots, quickly turned to the color and warmth we associate with grave markers. Gloves were a rude joke that kept the hands damp and useless.

The serious goose hunter made several trips from the car or the buggy—one of which saw him carrying either a pail to burn charcoal, peat moss or hard coal, or, as likely, a kerosene lantern. These were placed between his knees and under the poncho or blanket. If you didn't recognize a goose hunter from his attitude and appurtenances, you could smell him out. Today, thanks be to whomever it was, a few hundred dollars worth of down—mittens, parka, muff, underwear, overalls, cap, dickey and socks—serve well enough to keep the gunner both alive and mobile in all but the most severe conditions.

Now we see the serious goose hunter seated in the blind—exhausted after his several trips—for he needs sixty decoys, his lunch basket, heater, guns and shells, etc., each of which requires a separate journey. He is tired, not only from his predawn labor, but also from the fact that he has not had much sleep the night before. In camp between rounds of gin rummy, goose hunters discuss, in varying tones of voice, the essential details of the sport: guides, guns, loads, calls, decoy rigs, decoy sizes and the like.

About the best goose guide I ever saw was a man from upstate New York. First off, he wasn't bone lazy. Second, he *really* knew how to set out a rig in the way that geese

Moment of Rest
WHITE-FRONTED GEESE

would appreciate so that his gunners would be able to take birds both coming into and leaving the set. He understood wind and flight patterns, and *most* remarkable—he *really* knew how to call and, almost unbelievably, he knew when *not* to call. He did not call to impress gunners with the purity of his tone; he called to bring geese into gun range—that's all. Now I know that your experienced well-traveled goose hunter will say I'm lying and that no such paragon exists. And I realize that few of you have ever seen a guide who was not only willing, but eager, to put out about 200 decoys—at 3 a.m. *before you get into the blind*—and not to just arrive at the same identical set that had been there since opening day. Harold not only did that, but was willing and eager to shift the decoys as the flight patterns of the birds shifted. Yes—he actually *worked*—actually left the blind and went into the field. And further—and I know you won't believe this at all—he did not insist that he was the best shot, caller, etc., etc. And he didn't even carry a gun! When he went out after a cripple, he borrowed one . . . .

Now I know that you never had a guide like this. Harold is the only one I've ever even heard about. No—nothing on earth will get me to reveal his name or address. Harold is *mine*. Not mine alone—but as close to that as decency will permit.

For those of you who haven't suffered the *average* goose guide, I'll give you a thumbnail sketch. He puts out the smallest set of decoys that he can get by with—and the cheapest kind. He never moves them, weather changes and feeding patterns notwithstanding. He cannot call well and insists on calling constantly. If, by mistake, geese do circle the blind, he is the first one up shooting and claims at least one bird. If the geese flare from the set because he is too lazy to get the frost off the blocks, he

Breaking Weather—Canada Geese

blames you for looking up or fidgeting around. If your gun isn't nearly identical to his (God forbid!), he looks at it as if it were painted blaze orange. His dog is always out of control running around in the field, and he is either shouting at it or chasing it or both.

He is never in the blind when you need him—but always out in the open doing mysterious chores. He blames everything but himself for the poor shooting: You are there when the moon is wrong, the wind is wrong, and geese are either feeding somewhere else or at night or not at all. He often refers to himself as a "professional guide." I'll usually agree with the adjective—but not the noun.

A good goose guide, like the legendary Harold, knows these basic facts: There is virtually no such thing as too many decoys or decoys that are too big. He arranges the sets so that flocks have an open space, upwind, to come in to. He knows geese will almost never drop into the middle of decoys—they want a spot of their own at the start. He knows if geese are interested or not and judges his calling by the calling of the birds. He doesn't fool with huge flocks, and if a tremendous flight of birds circles over the stool, he lets them go quietly, because if you shoot into a flock of, let's say forty, birds, you've educated forty birds, and that's probably the last time any of them will stool. If you work on smaller flocks, you'll get good shooting over a longer period of time. He waits to call for shooting until he's pretty sure that you'll get shots at incoming birds and then have a chance to shoot again on the turn—to make sure that birds aren't hit and lost because they flew instantly out of range.

His blind is neat and clean—no candy wrappers and empty shells litter the ground. He moves the shooters around according to their ability—giving the poor shot the best chances and placing him where the better shots can back him up. He realizes that you are paying him good money and doesn't ask you to do his work: moving decoys or chasing wing-broken birds for half a mile. He is instructive, helpful, patient and understanding. He is also as rare as homemade bread.

It doesn't take long for the serious goose shooter to learn what the best goose gun is. A man who respects his game and knows the vagaries of wing shooting at waterfowl goes for the biggest thing he can handle. If you can't handle heavy artillery, you ought to think twice about gunning for Canada geese. You don't want to hear shot rattling off feathers—you want to hear your goose hit the ground, or you don't belong in a goose blind. A goose gun is a gun that will throw a tight pattern of 2's or 4's from the biggest magnum load you can stuff into it. Shoot one of the many fine automatics, or weight up a pump to ten or so pounds. You aren't carrying it around in heavy cover, so weight really becomes a factor of shooting comfort, not some writer's idea of "ideal."

For years I shot a 3-inch magnum pump—with a few alterations of my own. One was to replace the wooden plug in the magazine with a plug of stainless steel for weight. It kept down the muzzle jump and made it a better gun for tracking long leads on crossing shots; once you got that barrel swinging, it was almost impossible to stop. And the other thing I did was to shorten the stock about an inch and put a slip-on recoil pad over the original one. This gave me the chance to adjust for a lot of clothing in bitter-cold weather.

The thinking wing shot knows how far forty-five yards is—either by experience and what his eyes pick out on a bird at that distance, or he puts out a decoy at that distance for a marker. On overhead shots, he waits until he can see details in the feathers that tell him the bird is in range, or he lets it go. If there is a sadder sight than a badly-hit Canada limping through the sky because of a careless gunner, I don't know what it is. The careful shot doesn't try for a second bird until he's sure of the

Majestic Flight
EMPEROR GEESE

first. A second shot on top of the first one is virtually a rule for the conscientious hunter. Geese are harder to hit than they appear to be, but the experienced gunner knows that their large size means they fly faster than it seems, and that they are hard to bring down, even when well hit.

For a long time, a lot of so-called goose hunters have gone to large shot, BBs, various sizes of buckshot, and even homemade contrivances of wired shot, waxed shot and so on, in order to do what they shouldn't even have dreamed of—kill geese at eighty to one hundred yards. A bird as majestic as a goose deserves better than some nitwit pecking at him with a shotgun, hoping by blind chance to bring down a bird. The first deer I killed with a shotgun had two double-o buckshot in him at a range less than fifty yards: one in the heart and one in the rear leg. That's not what I consider a good-looking pattern for bird shooting.

There's no such thing as a goose gun that shoots too tight. I'd prefer a dense pattern of 2's, but generally settle for 4's because my favorite gun patterns them better. I'd like to try 3's, but like a lot of good old things, they're not around any more. Another

Winged Formation
CANADA GEESE

reason for my preferring 4's is that they do a fine job if a few ducks spend part of the day in the goose blinds, where 2's are just too widely spread for any consistency.

I'm sort of "homesick" for the fine old guns that were so superb for geese—those well-balanced, side-by-side eight and ten gauges. I suspect they left a lot less cripples for a couple of reasons. One was that they could do the job they were built for, and the men who used them knew how to point one. And I don't imagine a man did too much skylarking at ridiculous distances with a gun that spoke with so much authority at both ends. When you swung that old No. 8, you wanted something to happen and you were willing to take a little banging for what went on at the other end. You didn't shoot it too often just for the hell of it. But, the truth is that today's 3-inch, twelve-bore will do the job of the old 10-gauge. It just seems a shame that the big ones went out of style—emotionally, and even legally, in the case of the 8-gauge. Old Nash Buckingham knew what he was talking about when he said that "the best retriever was a 3-inch magnum."

I don't think it's "sporting" to be under-gunned for anything—from woodcock to waterfowl. I agree that small-bore shotguns have their place, but the goose blind is not one of them. A man setting out to gun the goose flights is under a moral responsibility to respect his birds to the greatest of his ability. I think that's true of all bird hunting—but the goose is the cathedral of nature, and we should approach him with a blend of awe and respect. I can never listen to an approaching flight and not think for a second about where he's been before he comes to me. The wings that carry him over my decoys have borne him through the high turbulent skies for many thousands of miles. He is part of a family group, chances are, and his far-heard chatterings are cautions to the young, encouragement to the older, and bits and pieces of advice to the flock in general.

If a lone honker, his neck swinging back and forth in his questioning flight, should come your way—think about him for a minute. He's an old fellow, more than likely the last of his kin. He's looking for a familiar voice or a small flock that will take him in. He's the one you often hear from farthest off—his lonely *heer-onk* drawn-out and somehow wistful in its plaintive tone... calling more out of hope than any other living thing that flies... knowing deep inside that there will be no answer, he still sends his echoing call to tell whoever hears that he is all alone. Old goose hunters and their guides feel shivers when these single birds fly overhead—they may not tell you why, but deep inside they know. Now, knowing you can reach out and touch this bird, this goose of many thousand miles, should bring responsibility with power. Do what you came to do, but do it well.

I like to gun the evening flights the best. I like to see one last chance against the setting sun without much care about the way the day of shooting ends. I like to leave the blind with the sound of honkers in my ear and see the cupped wings set and float this lovely bird to earth. The way to feel about the end of any gunning day is that something waits for you tomorrow.

As long as the honking of geese makes the sun come up, and we're there to be part of it—that's as good a reason to want to be anywhere that I know. And since I don't get out a gun as much as I'd like to, do me a small favor—miss one or two in my name.

WHEN PHEASANT SEASON WAS FROM CHORES 'TIL DARK

Pheasants in Fall
RING-NECKED PHEASANTS

You show me a picture of a cornfield pheasant and ask me what I might add, and I'll not delay a second in describing an overalled farm boy with a too-big pump or double and a sort of muddy-brown, long-haired, some-part Collie along to look after him.

No doubt most of us more or less remember our first duck or goose or grouse, but the first pheasant likely stands out as strong or stronger... especially if you were raised on a farm in pheasant country.

The thing about an old rooster is that he's smarter than most of us. He rambles around with the chickens when it suits him in the summer and then virtually disappears for the next six months come the first heavy frost. You can see him and hear him, of course, but only when he wants you to. Sneak up on him? Forget it.

There's a great appeal to the lack of ceremony in farm country pheasants. You come home from school, do the minimum of chores (fathers tend to look the other way on a boy in hunting season), take the gun out of the kitchen closet or the spring house, and get to it... with a jingling handful of heavy 6's for pocket music.

The fact that you know where they are, and have known all year, doesn't make it easy; nothing makes it easy with a wild ringneck who knows the farm better than you do. I don't really think that a smart rooster intentionally tries to scare you witless; it's just that's what he does best when he lets you see him closer than a half acre off. The first thing a youngster ought to learn if he's going to be a pheasant hunter is to be steady to flush!

One of the important jobs a farm dog has to undertake is to raise a boy. He has to accompany him on his chore rounds, trap lines, general excursions and hunting trips. In the times before yellow dragons swallowed up children and carried them away, the dog was allowed to follow him to school and wait outside until recess. (Some dogs I know became fairly reliable centerfielders in this way.) But the sight of a gun always made

Startled Ringneck
RING-NECKED PHEASANTS

the dog's eyes sparkle. I've always regretted not trying a dog named Freckles that I once owned, a dog that was a good deal of Border Collie, as a pheasant dog. She had a natural instinct for herding out Emdens and Pekins and no doubt would have caught the pheasant game in an afternoon or so. Instead I frittered away my time with an empty-headed English setter, who, if anything, was even more surprised than I was when I managed to down one of the three or four cocks that was my season's work; but she managed to look smug and assume part of the credit anyway.

It's nearly impossible to have anything approach the excitement I remember in setting out for an hour's hunt that carried me from twilight until after dusk in the swampy meadow where the pheasants roosted. Their evening calls were as evocative to me as an Angelus and did as much to make me believe in things I'll never understand as my twice-a-Sunday stints in our tiny white-clapboard Methodist church. That wild,

December Squall—Pheasants

demanding, imperial cackle has lost little of its power to make me stop and listen in wonder, awe, and, no doubt, a little envy.

No one can fault me for my admiration of the ruffed grouse, my affection for quail and woodcock—but I sincerely believe that the ringneck pheasant rooster is the smartest one of all. He has a regal bearing, boldness, and more than his share of brains. And his heart is as big as his pride. He'll fight a bird dog, or you, or whatever, when he's hurt; and those long effective spurs have made more than one would-be retriever a little skittish about messing with him.

He's a survivor. To the gunner his golden hues are as major a part of the autumn colors of our country as the oak and maple. I like to watch him strut and cock his eye at me—from sixty yards away, of course—saying, "Catch me if you can!" And, more often than not by a lot, I don't...which is absolutely fine by me.

SHOTGUNNERS FANCY: SHOTGUNNERS PLAIN

Heading for Cover
WILD TURKEYS

Shotgunning—that's what brings us here...to the prairies for sharptails, to the birches and alders for woodcock, to the overgrown orchards and hillside evergreens for grouse, to the farm country for pheasant, and to the soft air of the south for quail.

A shotgunner is a kid with a rope-slung croker sack humping along in barn boots with a hammer single-shot. He's a custom-booted tweed-hatted high-roller with a string of blue-ribbon pointers and a side-by-side with an English accent. Or a dappled turkey stalker with a 3-inch magnum full of heavy 4's and a wing-bone caller. He's a call-strung pump-gun ducker in a faded canvas coat that smells like a wet retriever, or a Yankee logger with his grandpa's Parker 16-gauge and a single-minded setter that knows this bird cover like her kennel. Mix them up, shake them around, put them in each other's place, change their clothes, do what you will, and it won't make much difference; bird hunters or shotgunners are all made of interchangeable parts.

They like the smell of wet dogs, wood smoke, and Hoppes #9...the look of burled walnut, old boots, patched coats and merry dogs. They discuss Parkers, LeFevers, L.C.'s, Hollands, Bosses, and Purdeys with the same reverence of tone that theologians use in invoking saints. They are all sorry they don't have an old 97, 12, 31 or 48 any more. They fuss over oil finishes, engraving, trigger pulls, height of comb, matt ribs and raised. They argue, lovingly and endlessly, over the advantages of cylinder versus improved, 26-inch barrels as opposed to 28, brush guns, pass-shooters, muzzle-light, butt-heavy, and 12's and 16's and 20's and 28's. Should any of those subjects lose vigor (not likely), there's always 8's or 9's or 7½'s; heavy 4's or 6's; and why don't they make 3's or 7's or 10's any more?

They heft and swing each other's guns through the old bird paintings over the fireplace and swear they couldn't miss with this one or that—and for the moment sincerely believe it. They rattle the dog whistles around their neck, fondle the duck and goose calls and compare pocketknives—the older the better. Up from the grave they summon old Bess, Tar, Buck, and Belle, with tales of valor and skill that would bring a blush to a Viking, never for a moment ceasing to scratch the ears and bellies and backsides of those whose turn at legends is still to come, pausing now and then to brush away a handful of dog hair from a shirt.

They treat a 20-year-old coat as if it were lacework, and britches that are falling apart at the seams are laid lovingly over the backs of chairs. The pointing-dog men

Misty Morning—Green-Winged Teal

Fast Formation
MOURNING DOVES

carry flushing whips, and the retriever men heavy leashes—both more symbolic than utilitarian—a statement of faith—ornaments of affiliation to match the pins and badges on their hats.

Names don't mean much when there are other things that identify a man—the one with the 21, the tri-color owner, the yellow-lab or the Chesapeake man. It's a semi-secret society, and you're not welcome without a shotgun; but you're family, a long-time friend, after one day together in the field when you're a gunner.

Should all go well and the man-in-the-boy or the boy-in-the-man bring home a turkey, or a brace or so of ducks or geese, or a handful of woodcock or quail, and present them to the lady of the house, common sense and experience tell her not to make a big thing about asking how it all went—because a real shotgunner will tell her. It might go something like this: "Well, Bill and I got up this morning about 3 o'clock. You remember Bill, don't you, Martha? He's the one with the Chesapeake named Sandy, the guy I told you about that shoots a 3-inch 1100 with a 30-inch barrel bored out to improved modified so it'll throw 70 per cent with an ounce-and-a-half of copper 4's. Well, we rushed around trying to get to the diner—the one I told you about that has such good scrapple—and Bill forgot his Olt—Olt's a goose call, Martha. Bill usually carries two, but one has a split reed. Anyway, I had my Faulk, and we no sooner got in the blind than this flight of six came our way. I jumped on the call and had them turned and coming in just right when Sandy got excited and knocked over Bill's coffee; naturally I thought they'd flare, so I stood up and worked the old Model 12 three times. I think, and Bill agrees with me, that if I'd had 2's instead of 4's and a full choke, about 40 points, I'd have got my limit right there instead of just the one bird.

Well, while Sandy was out running down my bird, guess what happened? I just had time to reload, this time with just one 4 in the chamber and then two 2's in the magazine, and here they came back! Just like a picture, wings all set and dropping down; you ought to come out with us one time, Martha—you'd love it; and then Bill hollers, 'Take 'em!'; and we both shoot, and just one bird drops.

"'You shoot?' Bill asks, just as the same time I ask him the same thing, and the two of us just sat there and laughed fit to make the tears come. Here it is almost 7:30, and we'd fired about nine times between us, and we've got two birds. You knew that Bill was runner-up at the skeet club championship, didn't you, Martha? Only beat me by

Winter Covey
HUNGARIAN PARTRIDGE

Drifting In
CHUKAR PARTRIDGE

Quail hunters are often disguised as something else: doctors, farmers, businessmen, or schoolboys. No matter that they come in all sizes and shapes, the biggest as well as the smallest, the young and the old, will each happily make a fool of himself to amuse a young bird dog; and all are perpetually capable of becoming tearily sentimental over a shotgun or affectionate for a battered old shellcase.

When quail hunters meet in the field, they introduce themselves by first making sure that they establish themselves as such; names, professions, and hometowns can wait their turn until later, which is as it should be. If, for instance, you see a man working a soft-footed little lemon-ticked pointer (or it may be the other way around!), it's the epitome of politeness to open the meeting with something like, "Mister, I'd be real proud if I was you, that's about as nice a looking quailer as I've seen in these parts for quite awhile . . . Could it be that I see a little of old Lucky Strike in her?" This establishes both of you as men of discernment; it proves a common bond and gives you something to chat about—sort of a neutral corner while you look each other over. Is the hat nicely weathered, is the vest one that was given a little thought, are the boots properly aged and cared for? It is the sum of parts like these that add up to the man.

Quail hunters are big on manners. Good manners, call them traditions if you like, are tried and true safety measures—both physical and social. A gunning partner who never, never shoots on your side of a covey rise is never, never going to throw a gun up so you might have to look down the muzzles. He doesn't shoot low birds because some young dogs think they can fly, too; and as far as I know, no one has ever come up with the right thing to say after you've shot another man's dog, no matter how lightly. Good manners cover always knowing where everyone else is, whose turn it is to shoot, and marking down hit birds.

It's polite to make a comment on a fine shot and even more so not to say anything when what should have been a bird in the bag goes untouched. Gentlemen never "work" another man's dog unless asked to, and if you comment on someone's dog, see to it that it's close to flattery. Quail hunting isn't a shooting contest, or shouldn't be. It's more a play, where the principals are bird and bird dog, with the gunner as a now-and-then participating part of the audience. I take as much pleasure as anyone in pulling a trigger ... but I try to remember that I'm the last act in a three-act play and not really necessary for it to be a success.

Among the Pines—Quail

Of course, place plays a great part. The greenbriar and honeysuckle of South Carolina provide completely different gunning situations than those you'll find in the open covers of Texas or Oklahoma. I well remember a three-day hunt in a huge tract of heavy swamp cover behind four fine working dogs. At the end of the hunt we estimated that we'd *seen* two hundred birds, heard half again that many or more, but I'd only had one decent shot, and the others not much more. It was as close to hunting at night in a jungle as I can imagine; and having done it once, it quickly came off the list of places to ever see again.

Few of us really remember the birds we've taken nearly as well or readily as we remember a dog's first point, the fine retrieves, or any of the thousands of little things that stick in the mind with that sweet glue of pleasure. One of the things I remember best about a hunt in Virginia is that if you mix Cannonball or Brown Mule with Red Man and a little Copenhagen, you get a chew that's a constant delight. I think we did pretty well on the birds too, but I can't recall but one shot I made; and I wish I couldn't, because I have an uneasy feeling that it followed close on the heels of some offhand brag I let slip about how I'd learned to "paintbrush birds out of the sky."

I've been fortunate enough to have gunned with some absolutely magnificent shots and to have seen field dogs that were virtually peerless. But, there's always the interesting point of what's the best—an argument that I usually shy from—but since you insisted, I'll tell you. The best shot was a fat pecan farmer from Texas. He sort of wheezed when he walked, but I never saw anyone quicker or surer than he was with his 20-bore over-and-under. I'd love to match him up with one of the bird dogs that to me was incredible. She was a little plum-colored bitch of strange vintage and forebears (I suspect a pointer/setter dropper with a Gordon or Irish back a few generations), but she had it all, as they say in the fine print ads. It's a good thing she didn't belong to my pecan farmer friend—and a better thing for the quail gunners who share his part of Texas.

No doubt you've noticed that hunters and their dogs tend to be similar. You see a long-legged ribby pointer cutting up a field, and I'll bet he's followed by a gunner that's six-something and built like an axe handle. Your man of "average stature" is likely to be tagging after a Brittany or a three-quarter-sized setter. A man of my configuration, as it has been pointed out to me on occasion, would be pretty well matched-up with a Poland China or Duroc; but since philosophers teach us that most analogies are false, I tend to let those comments just slide. Besides, I have other qualifications that allow me to call myself a quail hunter. I enjoy a touch of bourbon when the dogs have been called in; can do justice to a tin of cornbread, if it's the kind with a little sugar mixed in; and can find something good to say about almost any bird dog.

Chances are we'd get along just fine. I usually have chewing tobacco, plenty of shells if you like 20-gauge 8's, and a fondness for a good story. I also have a slight tendency

Misty Morning—Quail

to get lost, so don't pay any attention if I insist I know just where we left the truck. We're probably just like most quail fanciers, a bit of a daydreamer with a touch of the wanderlust, who likes to hit just one more cover before dark. I'll wish I'd brought my other gun now and then, out loud, but inside I know that it really wouldn't have done much for my average. But I won't count your shots either, and I promise to remember doubles and just how your old dog showed us he could still get the job done. Like you, I'll carry home the image of a certain flush to tide me over until next time . . . the one where Honey stood silhouetted against the broomgrass, her nose searching out the first of the cooling evening breezes, and we watched her get it just perfect and then turn to look as if she half-expected us to applaud. I'd swear I saw a half-smile on her face . . . I'm not positive, but, after all, it's my picture; and that's just the way I want to remember it.

CREDITS

Manufacture supervised by William L. Cooksey
of Petersen Publishing Co., Los Angeles, California

Book Design by Richard Whiteman and Jack E. Stanley

Text composed in Century Schoolbook by Jack Cooke

Color-separation and film prepared by
Wild Wings, Inc., Lake City, Minnesota
and Brown & Bigelow, St. Paul, Minnesota

Printed by Jeffries Banknote Co., Los Angeles, California

Bound by Hiller Industries, Salt Lake City, Utah

Text sheets are Vicksburg Vellum Cover
by Simpson Lee, San Francisco, California